Let's Take Care of Our New Guinea Pig

Alejandro Algarra / Rosa M. Curto

BARRON'S

A very special present

Mark and Anna's parents want to bring a small pet home. They've thought about it very hard, consulted their friends, and have finally decided to buy a guinea pig. It's a very peaceful and tame animal, it's easy to look after, and it's also very pretty. What a great surprise for the children when they discovered they would be getting a pet! Or maybe two…

Many different guinea pigs

There are many different varieties of guinea pig. Some are just one color, such as white, black, golden, or silver. Others are a mixture of colors, with two or three colors combined, with small "patches" of color around their eyes, or the feet a different color from the rest of the body. They can also be distinguished by their coat. They usually have short hair, but others have long hair, cowlicks, or crests. Furthermore, they can have straight or curly hair. There's even a bald variety!

Let's go and get them!

The day has come to choose the guinea pigs. These little animals love company and so Anna and Mark are going to get a pair. In the store, they were advised to take two sister guinea pigs. The children didn't even take five minutes to choose their new pets. They liked two very young ones they saw in the show cage. The man in the store confirmed that they were "girls," and then after checking that they were healthy, he gave them to the children in a small carrying box. They couldn't wait to get home and put them in the cage they had prepared for them!

Preparing the guinea pigs' house

A few days before the guinea pigs arrived, Mark and Anna had spent some time preparing the place where they would live. For a couple of guinea pigs, you will need:

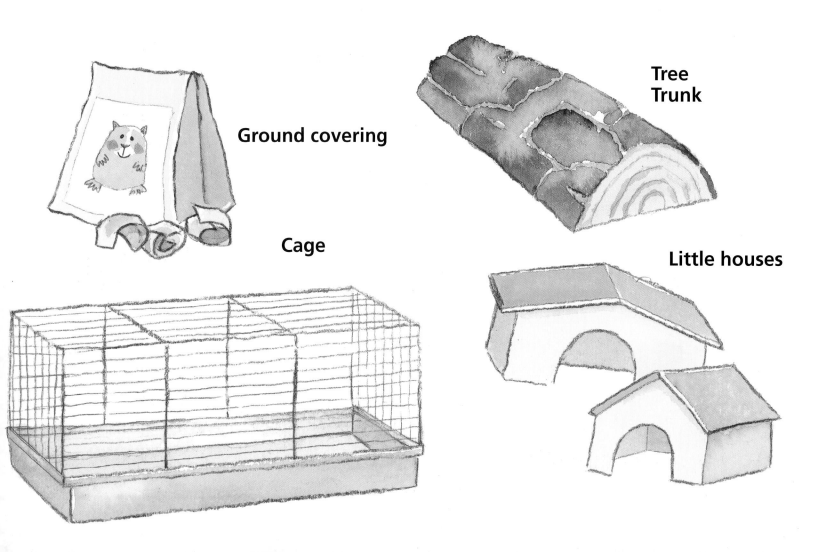

Ground covering

Tree Trunk

Cage

Little houses

- **A good cage or enclosure:** For two guinea pigs, an area of 11 square feet (1 sq. m) is ideal. It can be a typical cage or an open run high enough to prevent them from escaping.
- **Ground covering:** It's best to use non-aromatic wood shavings or shredded recycled paper. A 1-inch (3 cm) deep layer is adequate.
- **A little house for the guinea pigs:** It should ideally not have a floor, to facilitate cleaning.
- **A food bowl:** It should be heavy so that the guinea pigs can't knock it over.
- **A drinking bottle:** Inverted, with a special metal spout to stop all the water from coming out.

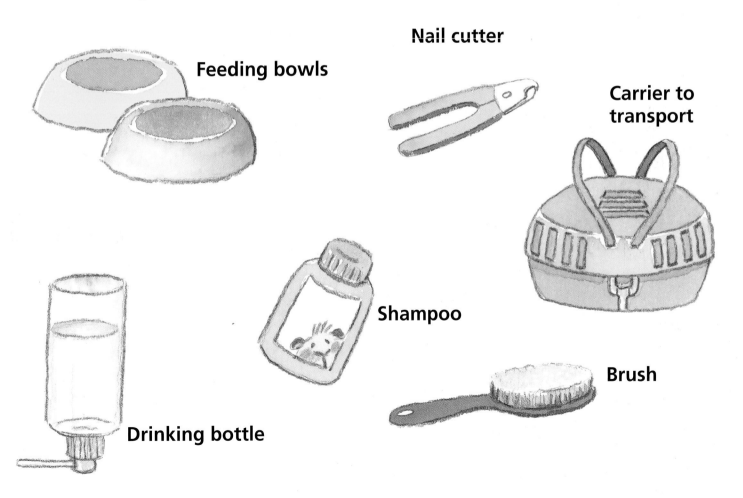

Feeding bowls

Nail cutter

Carrier to transport

Shampoo

Drinking bottle

Brush

First moments at home

As soon as they got home, Mark and Anna placed the guinea pigs in their new home. The time had come to name them. Mark called one of them Cookie. Then it was Anna's turn to choose the other one's name. "She's called Fluffy," said Anna, very convinced. The guinea pigs have short, straight hair. Cookie has a mixture of different colors: white, brown, and black.

Fluffy has black sides and a white forehead and nose. They both have round black eyes. "And what about their tails? Where are they?" asked Mark surprised. "They haven't got tails!" said Anna.

Time to eat!

Anna and Mark always make sure there's enough food in the guinea pigs' cage. They give them prepared food in the form of pellets and also fresh hay, which they love. They often eat carrots, spinach, and tomatoes, which are always well washed. They like eating strawberries, bananas, and pieces of apples and oranges, which contain a lot of vitamin C. They jump for joy when someone gives them parsley, one of their favorite delicacies. There is always fresh water in the drinking bottle every day, and the children ensure that the spout is clean.

Toys for the guinea pigs

There are many things in the cage, as well as the little houses, the food bowl, and drinking bottle. Mark has given them a branch. The guinea pigs use it for biting and filing down their little teeth that grow continuously.

He has also placed a wide tube that they like to go in and out of, hiding, chasing, and playing. They love to go inside a quilted cloth that Anna has given them. They play inside, stick their heads out, and watch the children from the edge of the cloth. How funny!

It's cleaning time

At the end of the day, Mark and Anna remove the fresh fruit and vegetables that the guinea pigs haven't finished, so that the cage is always kept clean. Every day, they change the wood chip bedding that covers the bottom of Cookie and Fluffy 's cage. Thus they ensure that they always walk over a clean floor free from poop and urine. Once every two weeks, they clean the cage thoroughly: the little houses, the bars, and walls. After removing the wood chips, they scrub the bottom and corners of the tray with a half-and-half mixture of water and white vinegar, to eliminate the traces of urine, and then wipe it dry with a cloth.

Fearlessly

Cookie and Fluffy are two very affectionate guinea pigs. They love seeing the children approach the cage, and they take the food they offer from their hands. The cage is placed in a well-illuminated place, but it is away from direct sunlight that might harm them. It should also be protected from drafts, which are dangerous for them. When a member of the family is nearby and calls out to the guinea pigs, they quickly stick their heads up and approach, or leave the little house if they're having a nap.

On my lap

The guinea pigs are not like other rodents that are more independent and quickly want to leave your hands to go and investigate everywhere. They like being picked up and stroked while they rest on your lap. Mark is too small, but Anna has already learned how to pick them up very carefully with both her hands. Then she sits down and places a cloth on her lap, in case the guinea pig decides to "go to the toilet" while she's stroking it. How peaceful and happy it is on her lap!

Our guinea pigs make little noises

Cookie and Fluffy make a lot of different noises to express their emotions and communicate with one another and also with Anna and Mark. The children can already distinguish their cries of happiness, anger, and pain. Sometimes, one of the guinea pigs gets angry with the other one and bites some of its hair so that its sister knows that it's angry, but they normally get along very well. When Anna has one of them on her lap, she tells Mark to come up and stroke it. What a funny noise it makes! That means it is very happy!

24

No! shouting

No!
abruptness

Be careful!

The guinea pigs are very tame and happy animals, but they're also very jumpy. You should be careful not to scare them. Any loud sound or quick movement scares them a lot. They're not very agile and cannot jump very well, so it's very important not to place them on a table or bed. Imagine how they might hurt themselves if they suddenly got frightened and jumped on the ground!

They might damage a leg or other parts of their body. Whenever Anna takes the guinea pigs out of their cage, she places them on her lap or on the ground.

No! placing on the table

No! placing on the bed

Let's get some exercise!

Cookie and Fluffy need to get some exercise outside the cage every day. In Mark and Anna's house, there's a room without any openings or furniture like armchairs or refrigerators where they might get trapped. The electrical cables are also out of reach, as they might try to bite them, which would be deadly for them. The children let them out every afternoon, so that they can spend some time running around in the room, investigating everything. This is very good for their health, and they are very happy when they go outside of the cage.

Bath time!

Anna and Mark brush their guinea pigs to keep them clean and only bathe them when they're very dirty. They behave very well and aren't at all afraid of water. First, some warm water must be prepared, so that they don't get burned.

It should not be higher than their necks, to prevent soap getting on their faces and especially into their eyes. Using a gentle shampoo they bought in the pet store, Anna carefully washes the two guinea pigs while Mark helps her. Then they rinse them and dry them with cotton cloths. How clean the guinea pigs are!

Some very happy guinea pigs

How happy Cookie and Fluffy are thanks to Anna and Mark's care! They never run out of food and are in good health because they get exercise and are protected at all times. Everything is a joy for the little animals.

Also, the two children have learned to be responsible with their pets, keeping them well fed and taking care of their health. This great lesson has taught them to always respect animals. And in exchange, they receive all their affection and the little noises of joy the guinea pigs make when they stroke them!

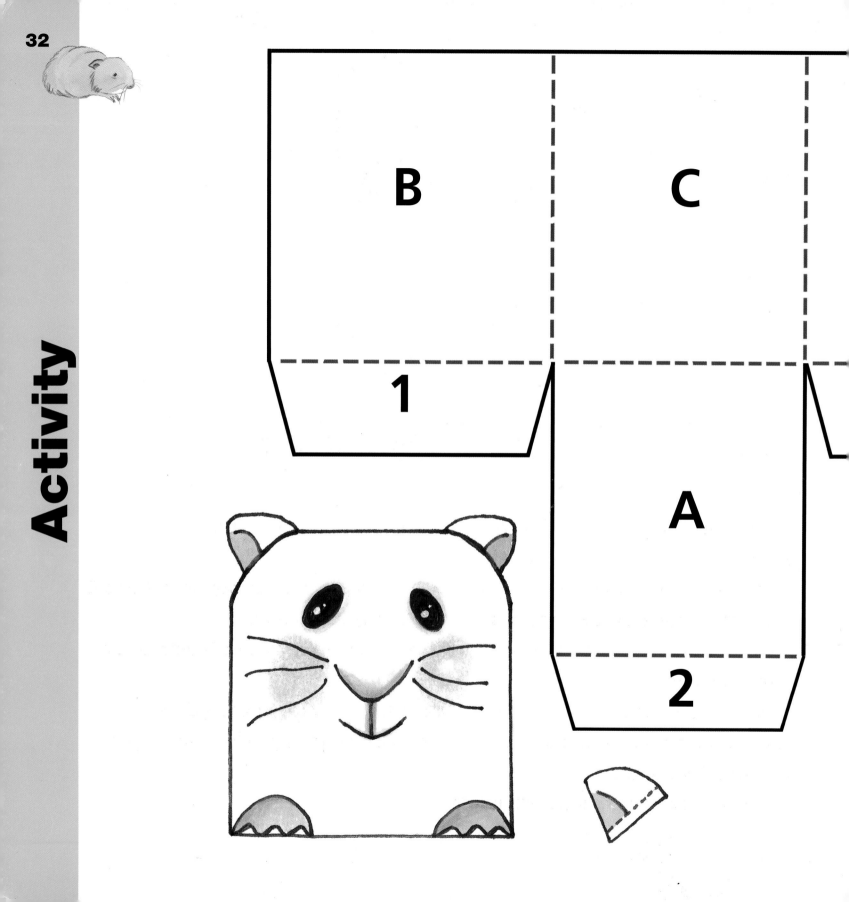

B

C

1

A

2

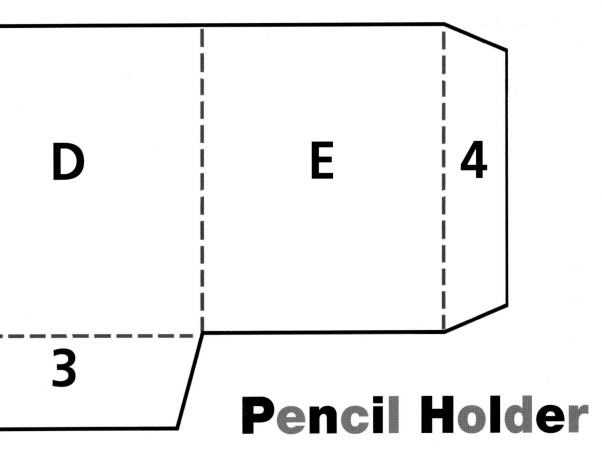

Pencil Holder

Material: Glue, white cardboard, a pencil, scissors, colored pens.

Steps:

1. Trace the pattern, considering that Sides B and D are the same; Sides A and C are the same as side E; Side A is the base of the pencil holder.
2. Cut out the pattern and fold it along the dotted lines. Line up B with D. Line up C with E.
3. Glue tabs 1 and 3 to base A. Glue tab 2 to side E. Glue tab 4 to side B.
4. Trace the outline of the guinea pig twice. Color it in as you like and glue it onto sides B and D.
5. Now you can put your pencils inside!

Advice from the veterinarian

RECOMMENDATIONS FOR CHOOSING YOUR PET

Guinea pigs are peaceful and tame pets. They love company and when they get used to their owners, they allow themselves to be picked up and stroked. Before buying or adopting a guinea pig, you should consider some advice. Guinea pigs usually live in groups, so it's best to have at least two. It's also better to have females, either two sisters or a mother and daughter. Two males might end up fighting, especially if they didn't grow up together. The worst combination is a male and a female, as guinea pigs can have up to five litters per year! It's important for the guinea pigs to be young when they arrive at your home, so they can get used to you while they're small. The stores that keep males and females separate are the most reliable ones. Thus, you'll avoid a surprise litter in a couple of months' time. When choosing your guinea pigs, make sure they have a healthy appearance, without any dirt at the back of their bodies or bald patches on their coats and with clean eyes and noses. They should be alert, but not become too nervous when you put them on your lap. Too much inactivity isn't a good sign either.

HOUSING

The guinea pigs' cage should be larger than that of a hamster or a mouse. The minimum dimensions are 24 inches (60 cm) long by 20 inches (50 cm) wide and 16 inches (40 cm) high, though the cage should be larger for two pets. Both open and closed cages are available for guinea pigs, as they can't jump. Open cages should only be used if there are no other pets in the house that might attack the guinea pigs, such as dogs, cats, or ferrets. Cages with grills on the floor should be avoided, as the guinea pigs can get their feet caught in them and get hurt. The cage should be in a quiet place. It's very important to avoid currents of air and direct sunlight. The most appropriate environmental temperature for guinea pigs is between 64° and 77°F (18° and 25°C). They are particularly affected by excess heat.

CAGE FEATURES

You should add several elements to your guinea pigs' cage. The floor should be covered with a 1-inch (3 cm) thick layer of non-aromatic wood shavings (white wood) or special bedding made from recycled paper. The following should be avoided: wood shavings from cedar and resinous trees (the aroma can harm your guinea pigs), sawdust (it's too dusty and can cause respiratory problems), newspaper (the ink is usually toxic), and sand for cats (it's too hard and provokes allergic reactions). You should also place a large inverted water bottle in the cage with a metal spout that cannot be nibbled at by the guinea pigs, as well as a heavy food bowl that cannot be knocked over, preferably made of stainless steel or ceramics, and a couple of little boxes or houses where they can take shelter in the night or when they feel scared. You should place some hay in the little houses, so they can build a nest. You could add a tube wide enough for them to pass though, a ramp, stairs, or another element they can use for exercising. The use of hamster wheels and balls is totally inadvisable.

CLEANING TASKS

Guinea pigs are quite clean animals, but you should make sure that their cage is always in a hygienic condition. The layer of wood chips should be changed every two to three days at the most, to prevent it from smelling of your guinea pigs' urine and poop. You should remove any fresh food, such as fruit and vegetable remains, every day. The water must also be changed daily. Every two or three weeks, you should carry out general cleaning: Completely change the wood chips, clean the tray with a gentle soap or a mixture of equal parts of water and white vinegar, paying special attention to the area where they usually urinate. After rinsing it well, allow it to dry before replacing the layer of wood chips. You should make sure there aren't any food remains stuck to the drinking spout. Always keep this area clean, as bacteria can thrive there and your pets might get sick from drinking the water.

FEEDING

Guinea pigs are completely herbivorous. One characteristic they share with human beings is their inability to synthesize their own vitamin C. Just like us, they need a diet that provides them with a daily source rich in vitamin C to remain healthy. If your guinea pigs' diet includes enough fresh food, it probably shouldn't be necessary to add this vitamin. If necessary, you can give it to them in a liquid form, by adding it to their water; however, because it deteriorates quickly the water should be changed daily. Another option is to give it to them in the form of crushed tablets scattered over their food. Follow the manufacturer's guidelines to avoid exceeding the recommended dose. The guinea pigs' basic foods are fresh pellets, special fodder for guinea pigs, and fresh hay. As a source of vitamins, you can give them a little fruit and vegetables, though you should always remove the seeds and pips, as they can be toxic. Iceberg-type lettuce is not recommended, as it contains a lot of water and can cause diarrhea. They love alfalfa, but you shouldn't give them too much, as it contains a lot of calcium, which can lead to urination problems. Spinach, parsley, and dandelion greens are advisable. Carrots are good for them to gnaw on and to keep their teeth healthy. Fresh food should be replaced every day. You should make sure they don't eat too much, to prevent them from becoming obese. Don't worry if you see your guinea pigs eating their poops from time to time. This is normal and necessary for them to digest their food well.

BASIC CARE

Both the guinea pigs' claws and teeth grow continuously throughout their lives. You should place a branch or piece of wood in the cage for them to bite and gnaw on, to keep their teeth within the normal size range. Ask an adult to cut their claws if they get too long. It's important to prevent them from bending back and becoming embedded in their feet. Care should be taken to cut just the tip and avoid damaging the vein that is visible on each claw (this can be seen by holding the claws up to the light). If the guinea pigs have long hair or cowlicks, you should be particularly careful

when washing their coats. You can use a soft brush to comb their fur, like those used for cats. If your guinea pigs get very dirty, you can bathe them. Use warm water and a gentle shampoo for your pets. It's important for them not to get water or soap in their eyes. Dry them with a cotton cloth or towel and don't use a hair dryer. Normally, regular brushing is enough to keep them clean.

BEHAVIOR

Guinea pigs are very tame and quickly get used to their owners. You shouldn't shout when you're with them, as they are quite timid. If you hand-feed them, they'll soon get used to you and they'll let you pick them up easily. The smallest children of the household shouldn't be allowed to pick the guinea pigs up, because even falling from a low height can be fatal for them. To pick a guinea pig up, you should place one hand underneath its chest, just behind its front legs, and the other hand underneath its rear part. Carry it carefully and place it on your lap. You should put a towel or cloth under it to prevent any "little accidents" with their poop. If the guinea pig feels comfortable, it will let you stroke it and it will grunt with pleasure. You should never place it on a table or bed, as it could easily fall off and get hurt. If you want it to get some exercise, let it loose in a safe room, without cats or dogs or cables it might chew or gaps it could get through. You should always supervise it to make sure it doesn't get lost.

CHARACTERISTICS OF THE GUINEA PIG

The guinea pig emits a variety of different sounds. It uses them to communicate with other guinea pigs and to express its moods, how alert it is, fear, pleasure, heat, etc. They can reach 8–10 inches (20–25 cm) long and can weigh 28–52 ounces (800–1,500 g). They can live from four to seven years in captivity. There are many different varieties of guinea pig, with many different colors, a single color, or a combination of colors. They can also be identified according to their coat: long or short, straight, curly, or with swirls, etc.

LET'S TAKE CARE OF OUR NEW GUINEA PIG

English language version published by
Barron's Educational Series, Inc., 2008

Original title of the book in Catalan: *Una cobaya en casa*
© Copyright GEMSER PUBLICATIONS S.L., 2008
Barcelona, Spain
Author: Alejandro Algarra
Translator: Sally-Ann Hopwood
Illustrator: Rosa Maria Curto

All inquiries should be addressed to:
Barron's Educational Series, Inc.
250 Wireless Boulevard
Hauppauge, New York 11788
www.barronseduc.com

ISBN-13: 978-0-7641-4064-8
ISBN-10: 0-7641-4064-7

Library of Congress Catalog Card. No. 2008928706

Printed in China
9 8 7 6 5 4 3 2 1